AF583145

0 1 2 3 4
5 6 7 8 9
A B
C D E F G H
I J K L M N O P
Q R S T U V W X Y Z

Jenny The Hippo has fun learning the alphabet.

Jenny likes the letter A.

A

Avocado

Ant

Aunt

Alligator

Airplane

A

Astronaut

Apple

Anteater

Angel

Jenny likes the letter B.

B

Butterfly

Bus

Baseball

Basketball

Bike

Bear

Bee

Bananas

Bat

Jenny likes the letter C.

Jenny likes the letter D.

Jenny likes the letter E.

E

Elephant

E

Eagle

Eggplant

Eel

Evergreen

Egg

Jenny likes the letter F.

Jenny likes the letter G.

G

Gorilla

Glass

Giraffe

Goat

Guitar

G

Grapes

Grass

Jenny likes the letter H.

Jenny likes the letter I.

I

Ink

Iron

Ice

I LOVE MY SELF

Iguana

Ivy

Igloo

Insect

Icecream

I

Jenny likes the letter J.

Jenny likes the letter K.
K
kangaroo
Ketchup
Kite
Kettle
Key
Kiwi
Koala
Knife
Kayake
King

Jenny likes the letter L.

Jenny likes the letter M.
M
Musquito
Mouse
Monkey
$
Money
Music
Moose
M
Mask

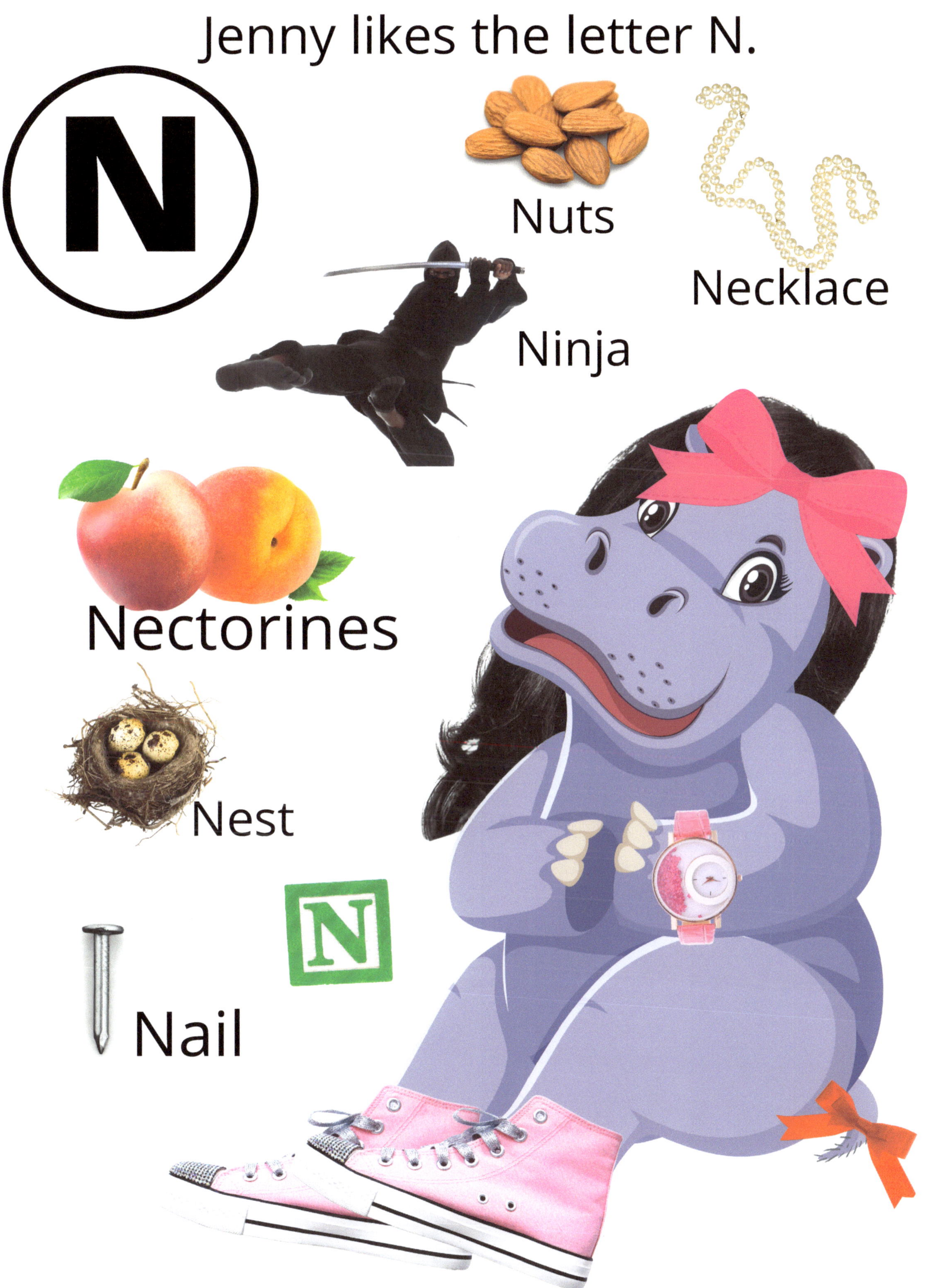
Jenny likes the letter N.
N
Nuts
Necklace
Ninja
Nectorines
Nest
N
Nail

Jenny likes the letter O.

Jenny likes the letter P.

P

Pot

Porcupine

Pears

Pen

Peppers Pickles

Plums

Pencil

Parrot

Peacock

Pumpkins

Jenny likes the letter Q.

Jenny likes the letter R.

Jenny likes the letter S.

Jenny likes the letter T.

Jenny likes the letter U.

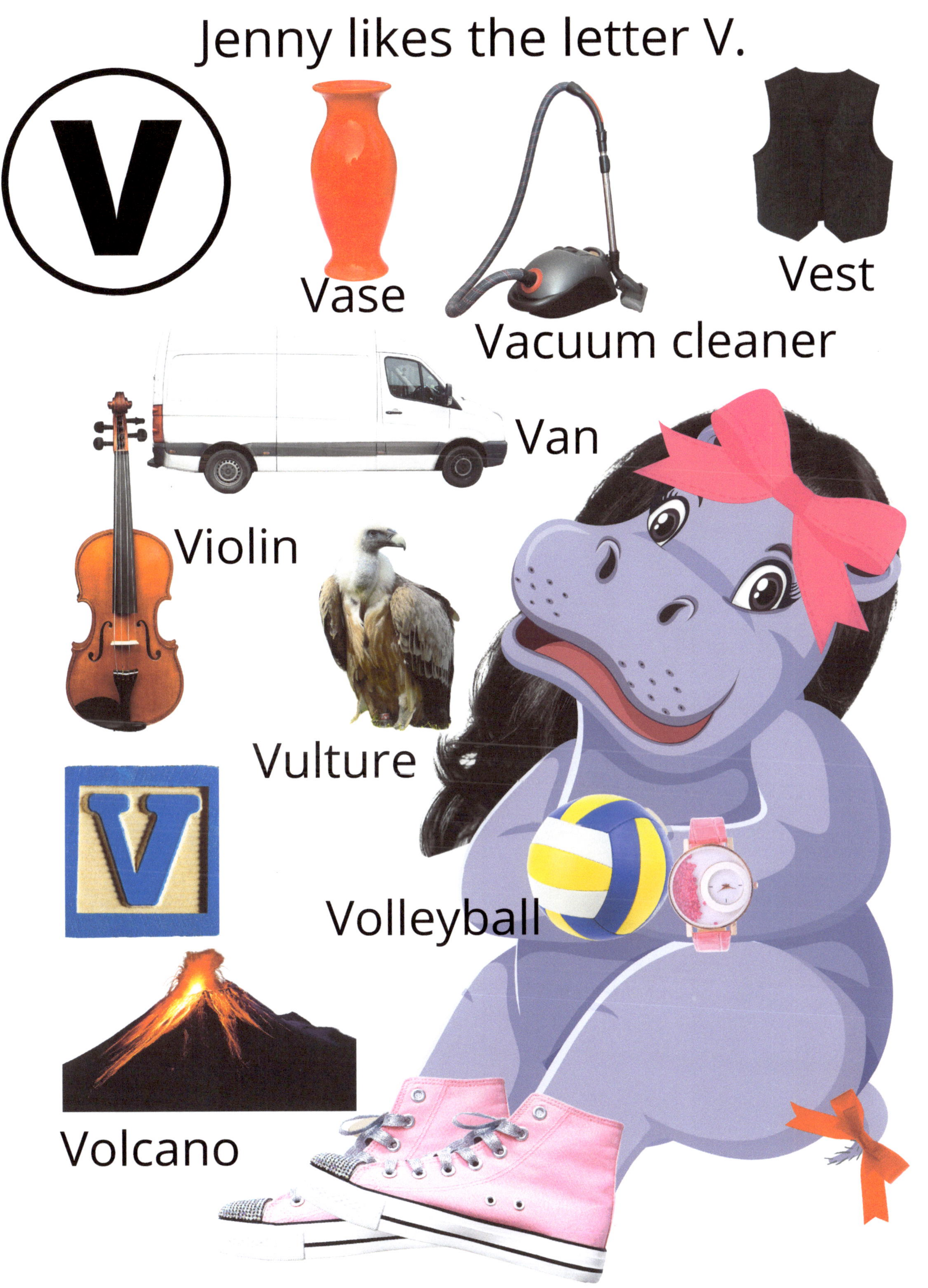
Jenny likes the letter V.
V
Vase
Vacuum cleaner
Vest
Van
Violin
Vulture
V
Volleyball
Volcano

Jenny likes the letter W.

Jenny likes the letter X.

Jenny likes the letter Y.

Jenny likes the letter Z.

Jenny had a fun time. .

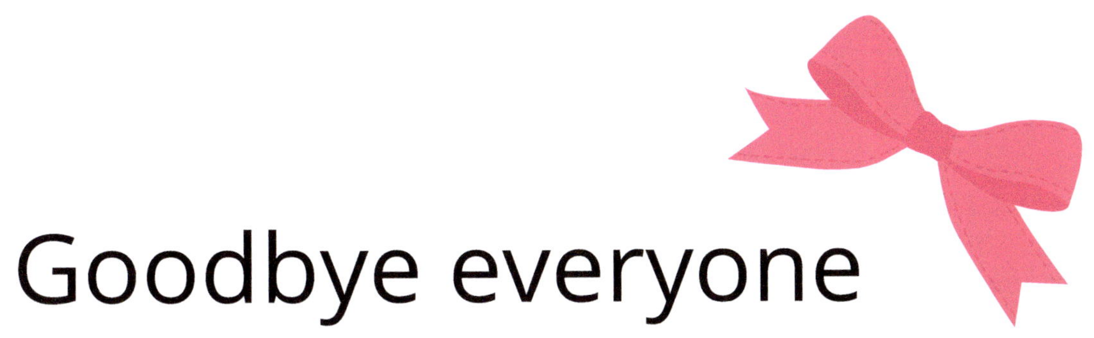

Goodbye everyone

www.ingramcontent.com/pod-product-compliance
Lightning Source LLC
LaVergne TN
LVHW071229160826
845679LV00003B/945

* 9 7 9 8 8 1 5 2 4 7 2 2 2 *